DEDICATED TO MY BROTHER
LAKAS SHIMIZU
(2005-2013)

Foreword

By Bayan Shimizu

(DO NOT SKIP THIS)

A pun is a play on words, in which a homophone is used. What is a homophone you (might) ask? A homophone is a word that sounds the same as another word, but has a different meaning. Related to a **plain** of grass and a **plane** in the sky. Here's another example. When you **search** for a good car make sure it's **Chrome**. [In case you didn't know, that was about the browser Google Chrome]. As you can see, a good pun can make you feel great because it is a playful use of language, and your mind compels you to laugh. As an author, making somebody laugh is a joy because it confirms that you can reach others and make them think through your ability to bend words.

Before, in elementary school, I wrote one pun every day. My teacher gave me space on the board to write a pun for the entire class to see. Every day, I came to school and took 10-30 minutes to think of a pun. I sat down on my desk and first thought of a homophone and turned that into a pun. My classmates really enjoyed it. On Valentine's Day and on the yearbooks during the last day of school, I wrote a special pun for each of them. Even today, my friends from elementary school tell me they miss my puns. Their laughter and enjoyment inspired me to write this book. I tried to make as many puns as I could, and that brought me to more than 100 puns that met my criteria for excellence.

It is both very challenging and fun to write puns. There are limited homophones, so there are also limited puns. You can't repeat a pun too much, because otherwise that pun will be very old, and people won't care for it, and then you have one less pun to use. So in this book, I never repeat a pun. What is so great about writing a pun is not only the feeling of accomplishment you get but also that you learn about how words have many meanings. If you think you know all the words, you may not actually know all the meanings. So puns really show the power of language as more complex and diverse than you may have expected. This is why it is fun to make the pun: you are exposing the power of language.

I wanted to write this book for my brother Lakas, who would have loved to read this and laugh at every pun. I was very close to my brother who died unexpectedly from a common virus that attacked his heart. While he was alive, we would never stop talking about one thing for entire days. He is forever in my heart. I wanted to see my brother in my writing and asked one of his best friends' mom to draw pictures of Lakas enacting my puns. I thank Mrs. Lin, who knew my brother Lakas well, and who made every illustration of Lakas. She portrayed Lakas very well. He was full of energy and for him to be in my book brings him back to me.

In between the puns, there is some space if you want to make your own drawing. I encourage you to do it because it makes the puns really come alive in your own way, but you don't have to because you see the images in your own head anyway.

To write <u>PUNishment</u>, I worked on it 1-3 times a week for 10 weeks while I was in Sydney, Australia. I would go into the office and write down 10 puns a day. I would not stop until I met that goal. Every time I was half way done, I did have to take a break for relaxation because my brain was working so hard to think of puns. I knew I was truly finished when I reached over 100 excellent and exquisite puns.

After the book was finished, I did research by going to bookstores both in Australia and where I live in California to see what my competition was. I saw that there were not many books with good puns out there in the world. I then brought it to a publishing company. When you bring it to a publishing company, you may or may not have it published because you might not like the way they would publish your book. I enjoyed meeting with an editor who loved my book. I eventually decided to publish the book under my own company, Soken

Studios. My friend Pauline helped me design the cover. My mom and dad formatted the book. Thank you for your help!

I started Soken Studios when I was 9 years old. I first created office supplies out of recycled paper and sold it to my friends. Now I publish books and create other products like video games and apps. Thank you for supporting my work by buying this book.

A portion of the money made on PUNishment will go to the Lakas Shimizu Philanthropy Fund, which supports the education of underprivileged children.

Now, What You've Been Waiting For...

The Puns.

WARNING

IF you are caught using these puns and saying you made them, EXTREME FORCES OF *PUN*ishment WILL BE USED.

PUN If you work <u>underground</u>, join the army! You'll be a major instead of a <u>minor</u>.

PUN When making <u>locks</u>, focus is <u>key.</u>

PUN Lots of <u>surfboards</u> were stolen recently. It was a sudden crime <u>wave</u>.

PUN In an <u>electrical war</u>, beware when the enemy yells "<u>Charge</u>"!

PUN Part 2 of pun: The first to do so will <u>surge</u> ahead!

PUN If you're going to be a <u>pupil</u> at school, you need to have an <u>eye</u> for trouble.

PUN While in <u>the ocean</u>, if you explore it all and find no fish, you can't <u>sea.</u>

PUN Lots of people came to see a <u>golden snare</u>. But they kept getting caught in it! It's such a <u>tourist trap.</u>

PUN Someone was so focused on what the <u>future</u> would be like, that it <u>past</u> right by.

PUN If a person asks if you have <u>knowledge</u> of something, just say <u>know</u>!

PUN How do you tell a <u>fish</u> to have a good day? Answer: <u>Carpe</u> Diem!

PUN The doctor said there was something in my <u>ear</u>. I didn't think so, but now I know it's <u>hear.</u>

PUN The same doctor told me that I had something on my face. When it was removed, he said there were <u>tumor</u> things (two more).

PUN What did the <u>digital clock</u> say to the <u>grandfather clock</u>? Look grandpa, no hands!

PUN The canoeing team had to keep paddling, <u>oar</u> lose the race.

PUN To care for an animal that flies, it's quite a <u>birden</u>.

PUN (Double Pun) <u>Trees</u> make good friends. They're always <u>rooting</u> for you.

PUN (Double pun Part 2) Be nice to <u>trees</u>. When they're in trouble, it's bad if someone <u>leaves</u> them behind.

PUN A man got a boat for a <u>cheap price</u>. It was on <u>sail</u>.

PUN When there was a fork in the road, my friend said <u>not to go left</u>. I denied him, but now I know he was <u>right</u>.

PUN I just downloaded a <u>sprinting</u> game. Now I just have to <u>run</u> the program.

PUN If people <u>shove</u> you a lot, don't let them <u>push</u> you around.

PUN Whenever I get a new <u>car</u>, most of the salesmen <u>drive me up a wall</u>.

PUN After <u>hang-gliding</u>, I felt really <u>soar</u>.

PUN The way to get a <u>bush</u> the way you want it to look requires <u>shear</u> power.

PUN I don't remember the second to last letter of the <u>alphabet</u>. I really wonder <u>Y</u>.

PUN When people realized paperclips were <u>conductors of electricity</u>, many people were <u>shocked</u>.

PUN There was a kid who always got old things, even after losing an <u>arm</u>, he got a <u>hand-me-down</u>.

PUN Because two people are <u>twins</u>, they always wear the same shirt and <u>genes</u> as each other.

PUN When a <u>businessman</u> scientist put his brain in a robot, he realized that he was a <u>corporate drone</u>.

PUN When someone told me "I lost my <u>electrons</u>!" I asked, are you <u>positive</u>?

PUN I don't like <u>subtraction</u>. It makes me feel very <u>negative</u>.

PUN Two fish are in one <u>tank</u>. One says "You drive; I'll man the <u>gun</u>!"

PUN <u>Trees</u> can't be aggressive, so their <u>bark</u> is worse than their bite.

PUN Feeding horses bunches of <u>hay</u> was too extreme, so the care-person <u>bailed</u>.

PUN <u>Weather</u> you like it or not, it will <u>rain</u>.

PUN Two people in <u>suits</u> finished a race at the same time, ending in a <u>tie</u>.

PUN When <u>NASA</u> was first created, the idea of going to the moon already <u>skyrocketed</u>.

PUN The best way to weigh a <u>fish</u> is to use a <u>scale</u>.

PUN When someone who had never seen a <u>hurricane</u> before saw one, he was <u>blown</u> away.

PUN Who <u>nose</u> the reason you <u>sneeze</u>?

PUN The <u>construction</u> area was pretty far, but it was in my <u>site</u>.

PUN I remember a <u>medieval</u> soldier who only worked at <u>knight</u>.

PUN I have a pen pal who only has a <u>right</u> hand. I wonder where she <u>left</u> the other one.

PUN After the rookie sculptor accidently <u>shattered</u> a pot, he thought it was time to take a <u>break</u>.

PUN When writing <u>music</u>, you should take <u>notes</u>.

PUN To be a <u>conductor</u> you really have to <u>train</u>.

PUN Because the worker couldn't <u>make</u> the tower fast enough, he was <u>billed.</u>

PUN Numbers that aren't <u>divisible by 2</u> are quite <u>odd</u>.

PUN When they changed the main part of the <u>temple</u>, many people were disappointed that it was <u>altered</u>.

PUN When a <u>priest</u> had to tell his family that he was fired, he had a lack of <u>faith</u>.

PUN Painting in <u>pixels</u> takes a while. You have to do it <u>bit by bit</u>.

PUN When the gardener was told to <u>mow</u> the lawn fast, he <u>cut</u> to the chase.

PUN I can <u>reflect</u> on buying a <u>mirror</u>.

PUN After becoming a main character in a <u>play</u> 10 times in a row, Johnny was on a <u>role</u>.

PUN <u>Demolitionists</u> aren't the best. They make me want to <u>explode</u>.

PUN Because the lumberjack <u>cut</u> a tree down really fast, he couldn't believe what he <u>saw</u>.

PUN The <u>purse</u> salesman was getting good at selling his products, so he eventually had it in the <u>bag</u>.

PUN Large <u>computer</u> viruses can be deadly. They really <u>byte</u>.

PUN Do you like rolling <u>cubes</u>? Then try gaming. It's a <u>pair-a-dice</u>.

PUN Never go deep <u>underground</u> alone. You'll feel so <u>low</u>.

PUN If there is a bad <u>king</u>, don't let him <u>reign</u> on your parade.

PUN Someone admitted that he <u>dug</u> a ditch in the road, but he didn't tell the <u>hole</u> story.

PUN When the police started making <u>rules</u> that were bad for them, it was their <u>laws</u>.

PUN Someone that made <u>bagged snacks</u> was really mad. They really had a <u>chip</u> on their shoulder.

PUN Someone was selling original movie <u>cassettes</u>, but when people got suspicious, he proved them to be <u>reel</u>.

PUN The most important part of a railroad music orchestra is the <u>conductor</u>.

PUN When some people that hated a national park made a false claim that there was a ferocious <u>animal</u> there, the ranger couldn't <u>bear</u> to tell the truth.

PUN When swimming with <u>marine</u> mammals, you'll have a <u>whale</u> of a time.

PUN When an owner of a business saw a <u>billboard</u> for his shop that he didn't make, he knew it was a <u>sign</u> that something was up.

PUN When poor people who made <u>neck warmers</u> were invited to an all-you-can eat buffet, they <u>scarfed</u> it all down.

PUN After a <u>cleaning</u> device was tossed off a boat, it <u>washed</u> up on a beach.

PUN Cutting down <u>trees</u> is a job I <u>wood</u> do.

PUN When doing a <u>word</u> search for saints, the man realized all the words were a <u>cross</u>.

PUN When someone wanted a <u>mobile</u> device to call their friends, the shop said they didn't <u>cell phones</u>.

PUN At first I didn't like <u>heaters</u>. Then I started <u>warming up</u> to them.

PUN Because a shop was being closed down, I wanted to say <u>hi</u> and <u>buy</u> to all the items.

PUN When making a movie about <u>scissors</u>, you'll always hear the director yelling "<u>cut</u>!"

PUN Why anyone would cut down <u>trees</u> has got me <u>stumped</u>.

PUN Because the <u>night</u> was over and I had to get out of bed, I started <u>morning</u>.

PUN Someone in a prison was <u>polishing</u> something from a movie set. I didn't know what it was, until he was let out with a <u>clean slate</u>.

PUN After a <u>DJ</u> is done with his job, what does he say? "That's a <u>rap</u>!"

PUN When reading long, <u>medieval</u> <u>documents</u> on a PC, you always have to <u>scroll</u>.

PUN When writing with <u>chalk</u> on a black wall, you'll probably get <u>board</u>.

PUN I always have a <u>knead</u> for <u>bread</u>.

PUN I don't know <u>wear</u> the <u>clothes</u> store is.

PUN If you claim something <u>underground</u>, tell everyone "It's <u>mine</u>!"

PUN Because someone had so many <u>stones</u>, they thought they could <u>rock</u> the world.

PUN A bad baseball player would be a good bowler. They're always getting <u>strikes</u>.

PUN When someone was nearly pushed off a cliff, the ground <u>rotated</u> so the person who pushed fell off. It was a <u>twist</u> of fate.

PUN When trying to choose a <u>tool</u> for mining, it was hard to <u>pick</u>.

PUN After an <u>insane</u> person lost the lottery, he was <u>mad</u>.

PUN I wanted to make an <u>explosive</u>. They're the <u>bomb</u> these days.

PUN When someone wanted to try to be a <u>sniper</u> for the army, he thought he'd give it a <u>shot</u>.

PUN <u>Wizard</u> school isn't the best, but it had a great <u>staff</u>.

PUN The castle guard was also the <u>timekeeper</u>. He always <u>watches</u>.

I was going to get a book about <u>colors</u>, but I had <u>red</u> it already, just like you have done to this book.

About the Author:

Bayan Shimizu is 12 years old.

<u>PUNishment</u> is his first book.

About the Publisher:

Soken Studios produces books, video games, apps, and other projects.

Published in the United States by Soken Studios.
www.sokenstudios.com

ISBN 978-1505660340

Illustrations by Amy Lin.

Book Cover Design by Pauline Vo.

Made in the USA
Lexington, KY
27 June 2015